Original title:
Mushrooms and Mirth

Copyright © 2025 Creative Arts Management OÜ
All rights reserved.

Author: Sophia Kingsley
ISBN HARDBACK: 978-1-80567-261-6
ISBN PAPERBACK: 978-1-80567-560-0

Secrets Unveiled Beneath

In the shadows where whispers dwell,
Tiny cap and gills, they swell.
Under leaf and earthy bed,
They giggle softly, softly said.

Dancing spores in daylight glow,
Peeking past the roots below.
Each hidden joke, a hidden tease,
Nature's jesters rustle the leaves.

The Laughter of the Undergrowth

Beneath the ferns, a secret laugh,
Poking fun at nature's path.
A toadstool wears a jaunty cap,
While critters dance and sound the clap.

Frilly edges, a silly pose,
A ticklish breeze where no one knows.
Chasing shadows, they leap and twirl,
In this delight, both sweet and whirl.

Sprightly Stems

Tiny hats on slender necks,
Jesting with their quirky specs.
With every bump and every bound,
A laughter rises from the ground.

Wiggling beings with joy that spreads,
Each step a dance on forest beds.
Their stories told in giggles light,
As day turns soft from day to night.

The Joyful Entanglement

In tangled roots, a jest is shared,
Underneath a veil, none impaired.
Tickling trails of foggy air,
A merry dance without a care.

Laughter rolls on dewy ground,
With every twist, a grin is found.
These caps of color tease and play,
A sprightly jest - a bright bouquet!

Nature's Hidden Revels

In shaded nooks, they sprout with glee,
A cap and stem, a sight to see.
They dance and twirl in earthy grace,
A secret party in this place.

With polka dots in colors bright,
They giggle softly, what a sight!
Under the moss, they plot and scheme,
In this enchanted, fungal dream.

Joys Beneath the Leaves.

Beneath the leaves, a world unfolds,
Where silly shapes break nature's molds.
They tickle toes with spongy delight,
Inviting laughter in the night.

In woodland corners, jokes are shared,
The tiny caps, they never scared.
With every spore, a chuckle flies,
A secret world beneath the skies.

Fungi Whispers

Whispers of laughter in the damp,
In darkened woods, there's no wet stamp.
A mischief brewed in nature's pot,
These jolly caps, they jiggle a lot.

They wriggle and wobble, tease the air,
With friendly glee, they spread their flair.
From tiny blooms, the giggles flow,
In secret glades, they steal the show.

Joyful Spores

A sprinkle here, a dash of cheer,
With every puff, the fun draws near.
They cartwheel on the forest floor,
Inviting all to laugh and soar.

In shades of brown and purple hue,
These tiny jesters know what to do.
With every spore, a chuckle bright,
In nature's laughter, pure delight.

Underneath Umbrella Skies

Beneath the caps that twirl and sway,
Tiny dancers join the play.
With smiles big and joy to lend,
They giggle as the raindrops bend.

In colors bright, like candy dreams,
They splash and jump in sunny beams.
Each pop of laughter fills the air,
With silly hats and fun to spare.

Laughter in the Leaf Litter

Crispy crunch where creatures hide,
Giggling sounds spill out with pride.
Puppies chase while shadows glide,
Nature's stage where fun's supplied.

With twirls and spins, they jump about,
In rustling leaves, they dance and shout.
Tickles from the breeze they feel,
In their heart, it's all surreal.

Enchanted Mycelium

Beneath the ground, a secret spree,
Whispers of joy, just wait and see.
Fungi parties fill the night,
With glowing caps, oh what a sight!

Jolly friends in hats so spry,
Swaying gently, never shy.
With each soft laugh, the world spins round,
In hidden realms where fun is found.

Sips of Sunlight

Bright yellow caps drink in the sun,
Sharing stories, oh what fun!
Each sip brings giggles, sweet delight,
As day turns slowly into night.

With tiny cups that catch the rays,
They toast to life in playful ways.
Beneath the glow, wild spirits cheer,
In every laugh, the world draws near.

Beneath the Forest's Smile

In the woods where laughter grows,
Tiny caps wear smiling bows.
Jesters dance in hats so bright,
Spreading cheer from morn till night.

A tangle of fables, twist and twirl,
Each little sprout, a giggling pearl.
Nature's jesters, oh what a sight,
Tickling fancies, pure delight.

Giddy in the Shroomlight

Underneath the glow of the moon,
Frolicking fungi, a merry tune.
With every step, they jig and sway,
Green caps nodding, come out to play.

Giggles echo, soft and sweet,
While critters shuffle on tiny feet.
In the night, they twirl around,
A waltz of wonders, joy unbound.

Playful Shadows

Whispers of joy in the twilight haze,
Mischievous shadows perform their plays.
Caps like hats on all the ground,
In this kingdom, laughter's found.

Tickling the toes of the unsuspecting,
With each little hop, they're quite demanding.
Join the frolic; don't be shy,
Under this canopy where spirits fly.

The Cheerful Decay

Amidst the ruins, joy decays,
With every squish, a chuckle stays.
Fungi sprout in joyous bursts,
In this decay, no one thirsts.

The forest floor, a laugh parade,
Life springs forth from what has frayed.
In all things lost, laughter's key,
The charm of life, wild and free.

Underneath the Ferns

Beneath the leaves, they peek and play,
Dancing in shadows, come what may.
Cap and stem, a jovial crew,
Whispering secrets, just us two.

A squishy plop, the laughter grows,
Tickling toes and wiggling toes.
Swirling colors, a wobbly sight,
Muffled giggles, pure delight.

The Giggle of the Green

In the meadow, a chuckle blooms,
Tiny hats in splendid rooms.
Twirling caps on grassy hills,
Bouncing round with joyous thrills.

A friendly poke with a playful nudge,
Sprouting giggles that won't budge.
Fleeting pranks in the dappled light,
Nature's jesters, such a sight!

Surprise in the Shadows

In twilight's grasp, surprises leer,
Popping up, it's hard to steer.
A squeeze, a squish, a funny sound,
Expecting a laugh, joy abound.

Peek-a-boo beneath the trees,
Catch a snicker in the breeze.
Curly tops and wiggly stem,
Whispering tricks, my little gem.

Fungal Fête

A party sprung from dampened ground,
Jumping jollies all around.
Ribbons twirled in nature's hall,
Giddy giggles, come one, come all!

Twirling sprights in a colorful dance,
Whiskers twitching, they take a chance.
Toast to the night with cheeky cheer,
To silly fun, let's all draw near.

Spore-tales and Snickers

In damp, dark corners, secrets lie,
With caps like umbrellas, they reach for the sky.
Chasing the giggles that echo around,
These little jesters dance, without making a sound.

They whisper of legends, both silly and grand,
Creating a forest where laughter is planned.
With each little poke, there's a chuckle to share,
In the tales that sprout from the soft, leafy air.

Meadows of Play

In fields where the tummies rumble with glee,
Fungi pop up, oh so cheekily!
Teasing the critters who scamper about,
In a frolicsome dance, there's no shadow of doubt.

They tickle the toes of the dew-dripped grass,
Making the sun feel like it's part of the class.
With giggling streams and wildflowers bright,
These playful mischief-makers turn day into night.

The Jolly Grove

In a grove full of laughter and bright, twinkly lights,
Grows a patch of delight that sparks joy in all sights.
With polka-dotted caps that sway with the breeze,
They gleefully jiggle, making troubles appease.

With each silly shape and whimsical face,
They craft a concoction of joy and of grace.
As shadows dance lightly, they scatter their cheer,
These jolly companions are never austere.

Hidden Hilarity

Beneath the tall oaks, where whispers collide,
Lies a party of quirks that the forest can't hide.
Each little sprout hides a laugh or a smile,
Turning gloom into chuckles, they go the extra mile.

With caps full of secrets and jokes from the Earth,
They spread a contagion of warmth and of mirth.
In the hush of the night, when stars start to gleam,
These hidden delights weave a whimsical dream.

Enchanted Caps

In a forest filled with playful shades,
Tiny caps dance in sunny glades.
They wiggle and shake with glee and cheer,
Making the woodland critters draw near.

With polka dots and stripes so bright,
They giggle beneath the soft moonlight.
Tickling the toes of a passing hare,
Spreading laughter in the cool night air.

Each one whispers a silly jest,
Competing to be the very best.
A gathering where joy takes flight,
In the heart of this magical night.

Delight in the Underbrush

Under leaves where shadows play,
Funny friends come out to sway.
A frolic of colors, oh what a sight,
Tickling the earth in pure delight.

They chuckle when the critters pass,
Creating a carpet of green and brass.
With each tiny face, a grin so wide,
A secret party, no need to hide.

Raindrops fall and cause a splash,
The little folks come out in a dash.
It's here the forest holds its breath,
As laughter echoes with every step.

Secrets of the Woodlands

In the thicket where shadows bloom,
Lies a realm full of laughter and zoom.
With quirky hats and coats of green,
These little beings are quite the scene.

Each secret shared, a laugh resounds,
As woodland friends play without bounds.
They whisper stories, weave tales of fun,
Underneath the golden sun.

A riddle here, a giggle there,
They dance like they haven't a care.
When twilight falls, in laughter, they blend,
A joyful gathering, no start or end.

Euphoria in the Fungi

In the dusk, where wonders thrive,
A funny gathering comes alive.
Caps all around, some tall, some flat,
Wobbling, giggling—a jolly chat!

Oh, the tales they craft with flair,
Of dizzied deer and a froggy's air.
With each burble, a fresh tale's spun,
In a whimsical world where all is fun.

Bouncing spores like a joyous cheer,
Making the woodland creatures near.
This frolicsome party, without a frown,
Paints the forest in laughter's crown.

A Celebration of Clarity

Fungi frolic in the sun,
With polka dots, they dance and run.
Whispers of laughter fill the air,
As they twirl without a care.

Each cap a hat, each stem a shoe,
Wobbling wildly, oh what a zoo!
Giggles echo from hidden nooks,
As they read their fanciful books.

With jellybeans and sprinkles bright,
They feast beneath the moonlit night.
Riddles shared in joyous cheers,
Spreading laughter, soothing fears.

So raise a toast to the kind and spry,
In whimsical clothes, they leap and fly.
With joyous hearts, they charm the crowd,
Oh, what a sight, so merry and loud!

A Canopy of Cheer

Beneath the trees where shadows play,
　　The little hats are out to sway.
With giggles sweet, they sway like breeze,
　　Tickling limbs of sturdy trees.

A wobbly dance, with no set pace,
　　Mischievous smiles on every face.
In the canopy, the laughter swells,
As they spin around and cast their spells.

The sun peeks through like a silly tease,
　　As they tango with the buzzing bees.
With each step, joy takes new flight,
　　Amidst the wriggles of pure delight.

A world so bright, it glows like gold,
　　With stories short and memories bold.
Each mirthful hop, a starlit gleam,
In this realm of giggles and whimsy dream!

Ecstasy in the Earth

In the soil, a party brews,
Where nature spins its vibrant hues.
A raucous band of joyful freaks,
They play their tunes for happy geeks.

Dressed in colors, bold and bright,
They jiggle and jive with all their might.
With squishy sounds and bubbly laughs,
They dance on roots like playful chaffs.

The ground shakes with their merry song,
While critters hop and tag along.
Celebrating life beneath the ground,
Where whimsy and delight abound.

So join the shindig, take a chance,
In this dynamic underground dance.
With every cap, a chuckle bursts,
In ecstasy, nature quenches thirsts!

Giddiness in the Glades

In the glades where frisky creatures play,
Tiny hats sway in a silly ballet.
Round and round, they spin with glee,
As laughter rings, wild and free.

A sprinkle of joy in the dew-drenched grass,
Each leaping cap makes the merriment pass.
Joking and jesting, they shimmy and shake,
In this glorious world, no chance of a break.

Their giggles echo, a quirky song,
In harmony, they all belong.
With hands held high, they jump and shout,
In giddiness, there's never a doubt.

So join the spree, don't be afraid,
Let your worries get beautifully laid.
In glades of fun, we'll share the cheer,
With each little cap, the joy is clear!

Colorful Sprouts of Joy

In the woods where laughs abound,
Tiny caps peek from the ground.
Dance around in silly glee,
Nature's hats for you and me.

Lively spots of orange and green,
Sprinkled where the grass is seen.
Whispering secrets, oh so bright,
Sprouts of fun, a pure delight!

Bouncing bugs join in the spree,
Tickled toes, oh can't you see?
With a giggle and a skip,
Join the nature's wacky trip!

Every step reveals a thrill,
Cheerful faces, all with will.
Sprightly spirits fill the air,
In this magical affair!

Mycelial Mischief

Beneath the surface, life does play,
Silly antics day by day.
Tiny threads weave in a jest,
Playing hide and seek, the best!

A jolly prank, a fungal shake,
Pulling pranks, oh for goodness' sake!
With a chuckle they entwine,
Laughter echoes through the vine.

Colors swirl in jest and cheer,
Making merry, spreading sheer.
Underfoot, the jokes unfold,
Nature's tricks, stories told.

From the earth, a giggle sprouts,
O'er the ground where joy shouts.
Hidden mischief here and there,
Lively secrets everywhere!

The Whimsical Harvest

Picking colors from the ground,
Frolicsome fungi all around.
With a basket, laughter flows,
What a sight, a joyful show!

Chasing shadows, bright and bold,
Gathering stories yet untold.
Every patch, a funny tale,
In this harvest, joy won't fail.

Giggles rise with each great find,
Charmed by fun, hearts intertwined.
Nature's gift, a splendid guide,
In this dance, we take a ride!

Sprightly songs of life and cheer,
Lively moments woven here.
A tapestry of laughter spun,
In this field, we leap and run!

Forest Frolics

In the forest, laughter sings,
Joyful gifts that nature brings.
Dancing leaves and playful breeze,
Wiggle, giggle, move with ease!

Tiny caps that nod and sway,
Mischief thrives in bright array.
Bug-eyed beetles join the fun,
In this grove, we run and run!

Skipping stones and twirling hands,
In a world of jest, we stand.
Under boughs, our spirits soar,
What awaits? We laugh for more!

Frothy frolics in a line,
Each moment sweet, a grand design.
In wild spaces, joy's the theme,
Together we weave the dream!

Elysian Undertones

Beneath a cap of polka dots,
Cheerful sprites do leap and trot.
They giggle at the squirrels' dance,
In the glade, a light trance.

Tiny hats with colors bright,
Round and bouncy, pure delight.
They toss confetti made of leaves,
While the gentle breeze weaves.

A jester with a gnome's big grin,
Spinning tales of where they've been.
In their world of whimsy, spry,
Laughter floats up to the sky.

Underneath the waving trees,
Every secret whispers, "Please!"
Join the frolic, lose your woe,
In this realm where wonders grow.

Joyful Journeys in Greenery

With a spring in tiny feet,
Nature's laughter is a treat.
Tiny folks on broad-stemmed rides,
Through the fields, their laughter glides.

Bouncing on the fallen bark,
Every nook a hidden park.
They play hopscotch on a stone,
With giggles pure and brightly grown.

In the sunlight, shadows play,
Twirling gnomes both night and day.
Each new step, a dance to greet,
Tickling toes with nature's beat.

A stream reflects the joyous crew,
Every splash a sparkly hue.
Cupcakes made of dewy flakes,
Oh, the joy that laughter makes!

A Merry Gathering of Greens

Gather round, the greens convene,
In the shade, a funny scene.
Giggling under leafy art,
Each bright face a joyful heart.

Buttons popped with laughter's zest,
Every quip, the very best.
In the circle, stories spin,
Frolicsome tales that draw you in.

Sprightly fairies trade their jokes,
Tickling toes of friendly folk.
Wildflowers dance to the tune,
Swaying under the puffy moon.

A feast of berries, sweet and round,
Golden laughter fills the ground.
In this garden, cheer is free,
Join the mirth, come laugh with me!

The Hidden Celebration

In the shade where shadows play,
Fungi gather, bright and gay.
With tiny hats and silly grins,
They host a bash where laughter spins.

Chanting songs of joyous cheer,
Tickled twirls, they dance and veer.
With every jig, the forest sways,
As nature joins in funny plays.

A squirrel peeks, quite amazed,
At these antics, wonderfully crazed.
He drops his acorn, starts to clap,
In tune with the merry mishap.

So if you wander, stop and hear,
The giggles hidden ever near.
A festivity pure and bright,
In the woodland's dappled light.

Dance of the Sporelings

In a patch of velvet green,
Little caps are rarely seen.
They twirl and bounce, so full of glee,
In a mossy dress, they spin with me.

A wobbly waltz upon the floor,
Sliding sideways, wanting more.
Each step a giggle, each leap a cheer,
They nod and bow, no trace of fear.

With fairy dust and a sprinkle of fun,
They skip around, not yet done.
A chorus of chuckles fills the air,
In a whimsical world, without a care.

So join the dance, let laughter flow,
In this merry troupe, steal the show.
As night arrives, still brightly spun,
The sporelings twinkle, day's good run.

Forest Folly

Underneath the towering trees,
Where sunshine sips the playful breeze.
A gathering forms, all shapes and sizes,
Comedic sights bring sweet surprises.

With polka dots and silly hats,
They prance around like happy cats.
Elfin giggles echo wide,
As secret jokes contribute pride.

The wise old owl, with a knowing wink,
Watches as everyone starts to think.
A contest forms, who wears the best,
Silly attire, a wobbly fest.

At dusk, they feast on acorn pie,
With mushroom stew, oh me, oh my!
And as the stars begin to gleam,
They dream of joy, a whimsical theme.

Giggles in the Glade

Amidst the petals and the dew,
A playful scene begins to brew.
In a glade where laughter sings,
Comes frolicking fun on tiny wings.

They tumble down, a giggling heap,
As the fireflies begin to peep.
Their chatter fills the budding night,
With every flicker, pure delight.

A ladybug leads the parade,
In high spirits, never afraid.
Jumping jests and cheeky puns,
Among the crowd, the laughter runs.

The crickets join with a rhythm fine,
Their chirps a tune, a clever line.
As moonlight dances on the glade,
Giggles echo, memories made.

Tales from the Timberlands

In the woods where the giggles roam,
A toadstool hat found a little gnome.
He danced with glee 'neath the leafy shade,
While critters chuckled at the funny parade.

A squirrel wore glasses, too big for his face,
Told jokes about acorns with flair and grace.
The trees leaned in, with their branches wide,
As nature's laughter spread far and wide.

A raccoon with shoes did a cha-cha slide,
Tripped on a root, oh what a ride!
The fungi joined in, swaying in glee,
With giddy little spores, oh what a spree!

So gather around in the shade of the leaves,
For the stories that tickle, that laughter weaves.
In the heart of the forest, joy's never far,
Where whimsy rejoices, the quirkiest star.

Whimsical Wildlife

A fox in a tutu twirled with delight,
While birds in bow ties chirped tunes overnight.
They painted the woods in colors so bright,
A carnival of chuckles, what a sight!

A shy old badger wrote poems in rhyme,
With verses so silly—they stood the test of time.
The butterflies giggled, in vibrant array,
As they danced through the woods in a dandy display.

The deer wore a crown made of daisies and twine,
And pranced through the glades feeling simply divine.
With each playful step, they'd leap and they'd bound,
In a whirlwind of chuckles that echoed around.

So if you wander where the laughter grows,
Join creatures in revels, their secrets expose.
In this merry gathering where whimsy is fine,
Nature's own stage, a hilarious design!

Festivities in the Foliage

Beneath the trees where the shadows play,
The critters convene for a wild cabaret.
A hedgehog in sequins sang songs of the night,
While fireflies twinkled, a twinkly delight.

A parrot with flair sprawled wide on a limb,
With tales of adventure that never grew dim.
The laughter erupted like popcorn in air,
As friends gathered close in their revelry fair.

With daisies for crowns and vines as their thread,
They danced on the leaves, full of joy and dread.
For one little mouse, he stumbled and fell,
Yet laughter erupted, ringing like a bell.

So join in the fun, leave your worries behind,
In a world filled with giggles, where joy's well-defined.
For in the foliage lush, in this jubilant sphere,
The spirit of laughter is always near!

Jolly in the Jungle

In the heart of the jungle, oh what a sight,
Monkeys in hats swing with pure delight.
They juggle bananas to a bongo's beat,
While parrots squawk jokes that can't be beat.

Down by the river, a turtle in shades,
Splashing water with laughter, his antics cascades.
The geckos all giggled, clinging to trees,
In a riot of joy, they swayed with the breeze.

A flamingo tip-toed on one leg for fun,
Trying to balance—oh, what a run!
The jaguar chuckled, his stripes all a-flare,
As the party raged on with a colorful flair.

So come to the jungle where laughter runs free,
Where creatures unite with unbridled glee.
Amongst all the chaos, their hearts intertwined,
In a jolly adventure, true joy we find!

Beneath the Shady Grove

In the shade where laughter grows,
Little hats play peek-a-boo,
Tickled by the gentle breeze,
Dancing roots in a hidden cue.

With polka dots and colors bright,
They gossip in the twilight's glow,
Jokes exchanged in nature's play,
A giggle from the ground below.

Twirling in a joyous spree,
They roll like balls, so full of cheer,
A banquet for the woodland friends,
Where whimsy thrives, and grins appear.

So come and join the silly bunch,
Underneath the leafy dome,
With every step, a chuckle's found,
In the grove we call our home.

Capricious Caps

On the forest floor they prance,
With otherworldly shapes to see,
Each cap a hat of pure romance,
Chasing shadows with wild glee.

One twirls bright in a silly dance,
Insisting that it's royalty,
While another wears its polka pants,
Declaring: "Come join my tea!"

They whisper tales to passing bugs,
About a king who lost his crown,
And share a laugh through rain and hugs,
As sunbeams scatter all around.

With every spore, a punchline drops,
They scatter joy, they spread delight,
Keeping secrets where the laughter stops,
In the glade where day meets night.

The Comedy of Fungi

In the meadow, jokes abound,
Where funny friends sit side by side,
A treasure of humor underground,
As ticklish spores in laughter glide.

A tiny cap, a large opinion,
Claims it knows the silliest tune,
While the stout ones break out in minions,
Huddled up beneath the moon.

They ponder life, the root of all,
Why do some dance and others just sway?
And why does the tallest one feel so small,
As they laugh the silly night away?

So gather round, let merriment bloom,
In nature's theater, all are stars,
With giggles echoing through the gloom,
As humor threads through moss and bars.

Beneath the Earthly Veil

Where shadows play and giggles roam,
The hidden jesters twirl and twine,
With jokes embedded in rich loam,
They wink at creatures, feeling fine.

In earthy cloaks, they share their glee,
Beneath the surface, secrets spill,
With every squish, a jubilee,
In dampened mirth, the world stands still.

They cheer for rain, they toast to sun,
Adventurers in their secret ground,
With every spore, a silly pun,
The wisdom of the soft profound.

So tiptoe quiet, let laughter swell,
As nature's jesters take the stage,
In the earth's embrace, they weave their spell,
A rib-tickling, timeless page.

Fungi Revelry

In the forest where shadows play,
Little caps dance and sway.
They giggle and wiggle at dawn,
Their humor spills as daylight's drawn.

Round and round they twirl about,
With laughter only they can shout.
A jolly cap in polka dots,
Tells jokes that tickle and make us trot.

Beneath the trees, a kaleidoscope hue,
Each one sporting a unique view.
They huddle close in silly poses,
Creating a jest among the roses.

Serenading squirrels in leafy fray,
They hold their fun in a playful way.
When rain clouds rumble and thunder roars,
They just chuckle and count their spores.

Whispers of the Woodland

In a glen where secrets unfold,
Tiny hats of stories bold.
They whisper tales of the old and wise,
With giggles hidden from human eyes.

Among the ferns, they share a joke,
Spinning yarns that tickle the oak.
The fox, bemused, joins in the jest,
As laughter rings through nature's chest.

At dusk, they glow with shimmering sheen,
Making mischief in the twilight scene.
A comedic troupe in caps of green,
Performing skits like you've never seen.

As fireflies twinkle in the night,
They gather 'round, their hearts alight.
With every chuckle, their spirits soar,
Echoing fun forevermore.

Caps of Delight

In a patch where colors blend,
Jovial caps join hands, my friend.
A tight-knit crew of happy cheer,
Spreading giggles for all to hear.

With floppy tops and spindly legs,
They dance around like little dregs.
A burst of joy, a splash of glee,
Their dance invites you and me.

Hopping through the grassy fields,
They share the fun that nature yields.
With each footfall, a joke is born,
In the light of the joyful morn.

Dancing shadows under the moon,
Their frolic brings a merry tune.
And when the stars gleam overhead,
They'll laugh until they're snug in bed.

The Joyful Spores

Sprouting high from earthy beds,
They tickle the toes and tease the heads.
Poking fun in sunshine's glow,
As they sashay in a row.

With a popping laugh and a shimmy shake,
They toast to joy with every break.
A party hosted in nature's hall,
Come one, come all, to have a ball!

Beneath the trees, they play and prance,
Each one daring the next to dance.
With colorful caps, they strut and lay,
Spreading laughter throughout the day.

When the sun dips low and shadows creep,
They settle down in a giggling heap.
Dreaming of fun for tomorrow's score,
These little jesters always want more.

Nature's Gentle Grins

In shady spots where secrets dwell,
A cap peeks out, oh what a spell!
With polka dots in colors bright,
They giggle gently in the light.

A wiggle here, a wobble there,
They dance around without a care.
With every puff, a giggle shared,
Nature's laughter is declared.

Beneath the trees, they spread such cheer,
In woodland corners, far and near.
Each frilly edge and swaying sway,
Brings joy to all who pass their way.

In this green realm, the fun's no bluff,
With winks and nudges, quite enough!
So tip your hat and join the jest,
For in this world, we're all quite blessed.

Revelry in the Roots

Underneath where shadows creep,
A party starts, the critters leap.
With tiny hats and shoes that shine,
They toast to life with herbal wine.

A raucous cheer, a playful jest,
The underground's a merry fest.
With twirling tails and merry feet,
They celebrate with tasty treat.

The soil sings a joyous tune,
As laughter bubbles 'neath the moon.
In cozy nooks, the fun does rise,
With every sprout, a sweet surprise.

So lift your glass, rejoice in fun,
While revels last, til day is done.
In hidden realms, the joy is vast,
A rooty party, unsurpassed!

Toadstool Tango

With every step, they start to sway,
On cap and stem, they laugh and play.
With twinkling eyes and frilly feet,
They tango to the forest beat.

In the moonlight, shadows prance,
Each little spore joins in the dance.
A happy jig, they spin around,
In this lush grove where joy is found.

Chasing light and dodging shade,
They twirl and whirl, a grand parade.
With every dip, the humor flows,
Their playful spirit brightly glows.

So join the show, give it a whirl,
In nature's groove, let laughter unfurl!
With wiggles and giggles all night long,
In this festive place, we all belong.

Green Thumb Glee

Digging deep in soil so rich,
Where greens and colors brightly glitch.
A patch of joy, a splash of fun,
Where laughter sprouts with every pun.

With watering cans in hand we go,
To sprinkle love on seeds that grow.
Each tiny bud, a giggling muse,
In playful hues, we cannot lose.

With hands in dirt and smiles wide,
Every plant becomes a guide.
They twist and turn, a gleeful sight,
In every bloom, our hearts take flight.

So cultivate your joy each day,
In every garden, laughter play.
With green thumbs up, the world's aglee,
Tending to happiness we see.

Hidden Haikus of Happiness

Beneath the tall trees,
Caps dance in the soft light,
Tiny umbrellas,
Whispering wet giggles.

A gnome counts the heads,
Jumps back with a loud laugh,
Hats tip-toe away,
Nature's secret jesters.

In the shade they hide,
Spots of color abound,
Nature's stand-up show,
With spores that tickle noses.

In laughter they grow,
Nature's playful secrets,
Joy sprouted on soil,
From roots of the wild heart.

The Forest's Ecstatic Echo

Laughter in the leaves,
A chorus of delight,
Bouncing off the bark,
Witty tales in the air.

With each step they grin,
Twirling in playful dance,
Bright caps all around,
Echoes of glee abound.

Dancing in moonlight,
Shadows jive with charm,
Nature's quirky play,
Unruly, wild, and free.

Joy sprouts underfoot,
A merry little scene,
With every squishy step,
Giggles rise and return.

Celebrate the Subtle

In corners of woods,
Hidden wonders emerge,
Tiny smiles peek out,
Adventures await here.

A tickle from the ground,
Caps peer out with a cheer,
Surprises abound,
Joy we can't quite explain.

Whispers of the night,
Gentle chuckles arise,
A banquet of laughs,
Underneath the full moon.

Swinging light of dawn,
Dewdrops laugh on the grass,
Celebrate the joys,
Found in nature's embrace.

A Peal Among Foliage

A jester in green,
Amidst the leafy crowd,
Chortles escape caps,
Ribbons of joy take flight.

Soft rustle of fun,
Tickling the breezy air,
Laughter's hidden song,
Bubbles in earthy hugs.

Under the old oak,
Mischief turns up the fun,
With roots playing tricks,
And smiles growing with light.

All around they bounce,
Nature's curious jest,
A peal of delight,
In the shade, secrets fest.

Playful Peelings

In the forest, hats on heads,
Spots and stripes in leafy beds.
Giggles echo through the trees,
Tiny creatures dance with ease.

A cap of gold, a wink of glee,
The ground's a party, wild and free.
Twisting, turning, twirling round,
Laughter hushed by nature's sound.

With every step, a jiggle here,
A riddle sung for all to hear.
Whispers swirl where shadows play,
Joyful jesters, nature's sway.

When the rain begins to fall,
Silly slides and splashes call.
Underneath the boughs we crave,
Life's a giggle, love's a wave.

Ephemeral Revelations

Brightly painted, caps so bold,
Secret stories to be told.
Bouncing friends on velvet ground,
Where the laughter knows no bounds.

Twinkling lights and shadows sway,
Fungus jests in playful play.
Sprightly whispers share their tales,
As the evening light unveils.

In a wink, they fade away,
But the joy is here to stay.
Bubbles rise from grassy beds,
As giggles dance above our heads.

Each little cap, a silly grace,
Turns the world into a race.
Chasing giggles through the night,
With every twist, the heart takes flight.

Celestial Fungi Frolics

Dancing stars on tiny tops,
Nature's jest never stops.
Underneath the glowing moon,
Frogs join in, a merry tune.

Colorful caps on fairy feet,
Spinning laughter, oh so sweet.
Magic pulses through the air,
As the night sings without care.

In a patch where shadows creep,
Silly sprites and sprites who leap.
Whirling through the fragrant night,
Twinkling like a firefly's light.

With every step, a giggle bright,
In this dance, the world feels right.
To the rhythm of the night,
Let us join this pure delight.

The Secret Garden's Glee

In the garden, secrets bloom,
With giggles breaking through the gloom.
Petals whisper, roots delight,
Cheeky spirits take to flight.

Each hidden nook a joyful spot,
Where laughter dances, perfect plot.
Crisp and crunchy paths await,
Frolicking souls in joyous state.

Puffballs puffing, clouds of fun,
Chasing shadows, all will run.
Silly spirits in the sun,
Gather 'round till day is done.

With a hop, a skip, a jump,
Laughter echoes, nature's thump.
In this world of playful glee,
Life's a chance, come dance with me!

Glee in the Glade

In the glade, a cap did sway,
With tiny friends, they dance and play.
A comical sight, all dressed in cheer,
Their laughter echoes, loud and clear.

The sun peeks through the leafy crown,
As giggles rise, they never frown.
A bouncy sprout, a twisty stem,
They pull the pranks, a joyful gem.

With hats of brown and smiles so wide,
They twirl about, no need to hide.
A jolly band, so full of glee,
In the glade, they're wild and free.

When shadows play, they spin around,
A quirky hop upon the ground.
Each little cap, a jester's role,
In this paradise, they claim their soul.

Nature's Tender Jests

Among the leaves, a giggle grows,
A patch of caps with funny toes.
They wobble, fall, then bounce anew,
In this wild game, it's quite the zoo.

The breeze brings whispers, soft and sly,
As pranks unfold beneath the sky.
With every rustle, the bright folks tease,
A cheerful ruckus among the trees.

Round and round, they spin and hop,
With every giggle, they can't stop.
Their antics spark a merry spree,
Nature's jesters, wild and free.

A little rain, a puddle's gleam,
They jump right in, a joyful team.
With silly hats and smiles so wide,
In this grand jest, they take such pride.

Shady Laughs

Beneath the oaks, a secret band,
With spongy tops and playful hands.
They whisper jokes in leafy shade,
A giggly scheme that won't soon fade.

A bouncy leap, a silly jig,
As they waddle small, a happy gig.
With dappled light upon their heads,
They share their tales in cozy beds.

Each furry cap holds portly cheer,
As chuckles rise, we stop to hear.
They sway and dance, a jovial line,
In this paradise where sunbeams shine.

As night draws near, the fun won't quit,
They crack a joke, it's quite the hit.
With twinkling eyes, they bless the night,
In shadowed laughs, they find their light.

The Playful Forest Floor

Down below, where shadows dance,
A vibrant crew takes every chance.
With sticky feet and wobbling grace,
They twirl and spin, a funny race.

A puff of spores, a shifty grin,
As they giggle loud, the fun begins.
Among the roots, they seek delight,
In their secret world, they hold it tight.

A tiny cap, a skit, a splash,
They've got the moves, they're sure to dash.
With tickles blown on breezes soft,
Their laughs erupt, they're tumbling off.

In leafy lands where laughter grows,
The playful floor, a world of prose.
With merry hearts and twinkling flair,
They weave their tales, with joy to share.

The Twinkle of Tiny Things

In the forest where giggles bloom,
Little caps wait to share their room.
With spots and stripes, they dance in glee,
As shadows play beneath the tree.

A hat for ants, a seat for flies,
They welcome all with sparkling eyes.
A wild parade of wobbling feet,
In this land of laughter, oh what a treat!

The sun peeks through in cheeky beams,
Tickling fungi with playful seams.
Every squiggle, a silly prank,
As nature plays in colors blank.

So come, dear friend, and take a peek,
At all the nonsense, unique and sleek.
In the twinkle of tiny things,
Life has songs that the forest sings.

Festive Fungus

Beneath the ferns a shindig brews,
Where caps and stems share silly views.
They wear their hats, so bold and bright,
Planning a party by moonlight.

With laughter echoing through the trees,
They sway and shimmy with the breeze.
A conga line of bouncy spores,
Dancing wildly on forest floors.

Each twirl a giggle, a bouncy bounce,
Who knew that fungi could so pronounce?
With colors that tickle the senses so,
They leave us laughing, delighted to know.

Then with the dawn, the fun must pause,
Yet all return to their quiet cause.
Till the next night, they'll plot and scheme,
In the rhythm of nature's light-filled dream.

Cardamom Humors

In a patch where funny thoughts grow,
A dash of spice with a joyful glow.
Capers of joy in earthy delight,
Spreading laughter from morning till night.

A pinch of whimsy in every glance,
Offering critters a silly chance.
They twirl in the air, such lively charms,
In this garden where mirth never harms.

With whispers that tickle both soil and skin,
There's magic aplenty, let the fun begin!
A sprinkle of light on the laughter trail,
Where humor persists and will never pale.

So raise a cheer for the giddy shapes,
As they wiggle and jiggle without any scrapes.
In a world of spice, joy takes flight,
Delighting our senses, oh what a sight!

Light Beneath the Canopy

Amid the trees where shadows play,
Tiny giggles lead the way.
Bright little hats adorned with glee,
Sprouting smiles as far as we see.

A lighthearted group under leafy shade,
With jolly antics, none are dismayed.
Twirling and spinning in whimsical cheer,
For fun is the word that brings us near.

The thumping of beats from a wild toad,
Signals the start of a joyful road.
With twinkling eyes, they sway and glide,
Under the canopy, all hopes abide.

The sun peeks through with a chuckle low,
And winks at the fun that begins to flow.
In this enchanted forest, can't help but grin,
For laughter and joy are where we begin.

Cap-tivating Whimsy

In a forest of hats, oh what a sight,
Fungi are dancing, in pure delight.
Spot a red cap, it winks with glee,
Spinning in circles, just wait and see.

With polka dots bright, they put on a show,
Twirling and giggling, stealing the glow.
Nature's little jokers, so full of cheer,
They tickle the earth with laughter sincere.

A parade of fun, each step a surprise,
Their laughter erupts under wide-open skies.
Come join the fest, bring your best whim,
Among these fine fellows, your worries grow slim.

Popping up joy, like bubbles in air,
Spreading their charm, everywhere.
So take off your hat, and join in the play,
In this magical world, let laughter stay!

Brimming with Life

In a garden of giggles, the colors combine,
Fungi like friends, in a dress so fine.
They sprout like secrets, hidden from sight,
With whispers of joy, they dance in the light.

Tickling the soil, they wiggle and sway,
Living their best life, come join the fray.
Each cap a hat, for a whimsical crew,
They laugh at the clouds, as all creatures do.

In shades of the sunset, they chuckle and play,
Waving their stems as if to say,
Life's a wild game, let's relish the fun,
Beneath the big sky, our worries are none.

With friends all around, the party begins,
Each cap is a smile, and joy always wins.
So skip through the field, giggling along,
Together we sing the earth's silly song!

A Tryst with the Toadstool

Oh gather around, hear the stories they tell,
Of toadstools and chuckles, in lands where they dwell.
With caps like umbrellas, they hide from the rain,
Sharing silly secrets, never mundane.

Two pals on a stroll near a stout little mound,
Stumble upon laughter, joy all around.
The toadstools are wise, with each giggle they share,
Their humor contagious, a balm for despair.

A jester named Cap, in vibrant attire,
Makes everyone laugh, from the meek to the choir.
With humor at hand, they twirl through the air,
Spreading delight, it's a wonderful affair!

So let us rejoice, in this world full of cheer,
For every small laugh, brings us all near.
With friends in the garden, come share the fun,
In a tryst with the toadstool, our hearts run!

Nature's Chuckle

Under the trees, where the shadows play,
Lies a world full of laughter, come join the sway.
The ground's all alive, with secrets to share,
Watch out for pranks, if you dare to stare!

With each little sprout, a giggle doth rise,
Wobbling and bouncing, beneath sunny skies.
Here humor is light, like dandelion fluff,
Turning the mundane into truly enough.

They shimmer and dance, in a curious way,
Whispers of fun in the bright light of day.
Oh how they chuckle, these merry little friends,
Inviting all creatures, where the laughter extends!

So come take a trip, and stroll through the green,
Where nature's own jesters frolic and preen.
Life's far too short for a frown or a sigh,
In this delightful realm, let's all laugh and fly!

Laughter Among the Leaves

In secret glades, where whispers play,
Bright caps of joy dance in a sway.
Tiny tops in a jolly row,
Sprinkling giggles where breezes blow.

With each step, a chuckle's found,
As silly sprites leap from the ground.
They tip their hats, a playful tease,
In the wild, they frolic with ease.

Gleeful grins on every face,
They hide and seek in their happy place.
A cheeky game, a garden show,
Lost in laughter, all aglow.

So come and dance, join the throng,
With nature's jesters, you can't go wrong.
In vivid hues of shades, they hide,
In jovial throngs, let joy abide.

Caps of Contentment

In a corner of the cheerful glen,
Fuzzy hats invite us in again.
They wiggle and giggle, oh what a sight,
Tickling us softly, pure delight.

They whisper secrets from the ground,
Each round cap with laughter's bound.
Their playful pranks, a wonderment,
In the sun's warm glow, they represent.

A picnic cheer, a feast of fun,
With every bite, they promise pun.
Beneath the trees, we sit with glee,
As caps of cheer surround the spree.

A chorus of chuckles in the air,
With joyful spirits everywhere.
In this gathering, no sorrows remain,
Just hearty giggles that softly reign.

Fungal Revelry

Beneath the twinkling, starry night,
Little caps glow, oh what a sight!
They toss their heads, a frolicsome band,
Inviting all to take their stand.

Each face adorned with nature's bloom,
In revelry we dance, dispelling gloom.
A capering scene, where laughter ignites,
Whimsical shadows join in delights.

The moon laughs down on this joyous scene,
With silly pranks, all hearts convene.
They tip and twirl in a merry cheer,
Frolicking echoes, loud and clear.

So gather 'round, let festivities start,
With a wink and a grin, fill your heart.
In this realm of whimsy, we all partake,
A joyful gathering, make no mistake.

The Jester of the Woods

In the shade of branches, laughter rings,
A jester caper spins, and sings.
Polka dot hats on heads so spry,
With trickster smiles that never die.

They weave between roots, a laugh parade,
Playing hide and seek in dappled shade.
A jest, a quip, a playful tease,
The woods alive with joy and ease.

Little clowns on the forest floor,
Invite us to join in their uproar.
With nature's jesters leading the way,
We dance and giggle, come what may.

So lift your voice, let laughter soar,
With these merry beings, forever more.
In their whimsical world, we'll always stay,
For joy is the heart of their grand display.

Radiant Retreats

In shades of green, a party brews,
Caps like umbrellas, in vibrant hues.
They giggle with glee, on the forest floor,
Swaying to whispers, and tales of yore.

Beneath the tall trees, a secret fest,
With starlit toppings, they laugh with zest.
Each spore a joke, tossed in the air,
Nonsense aplenty, with joy to share.

The breeze plays tunes, a frolicsome sound,
Dancing and twirling, they skip all around.
A merry gathering, all shapes and sizes,
Nature's jesters, with endless surprises.

As night falls softly, they chuckle and cheer,
With moonlit laughter, they banish all fear.
In radiant retreats, where the wild things play,
The humor flows freely, come join the fray.

The Dance of the Vegetation

Among gentle ferns, a whimsical crowd,
In polka-dot coats, standing tall and proud.
They sway like dancers, in synchronized glee,
Two-stepping through shadows, just wait and see.

One's wearing stripes, a real funny sight,
Twirling and spinning, from morning to night.
A cap here, a stem there, they laugh and they sing,
Nature's own vaudeville, oh what joy they bring!

A tickle of laughter, as breezes entwine,
Giggling spores hop, in a merry design.
The roots join the fun, they wiggle and sway,
No worries around, just seize the day!

With every soft rustle, another tale told,
Of friendship and giggles, like treasures of gold.
In this dance of the flora, where joy meets the ground,
The beat of the forest, it's pure joy profound.

The Exuberance of Ephemerals

In a blink they appear, then they're gone, oh my!
With colors that dazzle, like paint in the sky.
A jolly parade, upon damp grassy beds,
With laughter and lightness, they bounce in their heads.

Up pops a jester, with polka-dot flair,
"Why don't we level up? Let's dance in the air!"
They flip and they flap, in the soft morning dew,
With every bright laugh, they invite me and you.

For a moment they shine, then softly they fade,
In the giggle of the night, their magic is played.
Oh fleeting delights, with a chuckle they wane,
But return every spring, just to cause us more gain.

It's a game of the moment, a jest in the woods,
Where joy is abundant, and laughter stands good.
In exuberance fleeting, they teach us to cheer,
For life is but laughter, so let's persevere!

A Symphony of Sprouts

In the morning light, a concert takes stage,
Little green wonders, in a bustling rage.
With each tiny stem, a note in the air,
Singing and swaying, without a care.

Flute of the fern, and the trumpet of grass,
The laughter of daisies, as moments pass.
A symphony builds, in the soft forest glow,
Watch all the gigglers, put on a great show.

The intrigued little critters, they gather around,
Entwined in the rhythm, such joy can be found.
With drumming of raindrops, a symphonic delight,
They dance in the chaos, till day turns to night.

So come raise a toast, with each sprout at play,
For laughter and music, we'll keep gloom at bay.
In this charming ballet, where the green spirits crowd,
A symphony of joy, echoing proud!

Laughing Under Canopies

Beneath the trees we gather round,
With caps of color all around.
We share our jokes and dance at will,
Among the shadows, joy can spill.

The squirrels join in with giggles bright,
As mushrooms sway in soft moonlight.
With every chuckle, we spread cheer,
In nature's arms, we shed all fear.

A friendly elf with tiny shoes,
Whispers secrets, shares the news.
His laughter rings like chimes in air,
Together we ensnare the flare.

So come, my friends, let laughter roll,
Under the canopy, that's our goal.
With every step upon this earth,
We find the joy in simple mirth.

The Secret Life of Mycelium

Beneath the ground, a party's planned,
A hidden world where fungi stand.
They whisper jokes in earthy tones,
As roots connect like chatty phones.

With every thread, the laughter flows,
A network full of silly prose.
They cheer for rain, they sing for sun,
In their domain, they have such fun!

A playful spore on a wild ride,
With ticklish shouts, it darts to hide.
In shadows deep, their antics soar,
With giggles echoing forevermore.

So heed the tales of what's below,
Where tiny treasures dance and glow.
In secret lives where jests unite,
The world of fungi sparkles bright.

Cap and Glee

The caps wear smiles, both big and wide,
In fields of green, they take great pride.
With every breeze, they sway and play,
In this whimsical ballet, hooray!

Jolly hats upon their heads,
In tiny gigs, their laughter spreads.
A joke or two exchanged with ease,
In this revelry among the trees.

With playful puffs of spore they dance,
Each twist and turn, a merry chance.
A jester's feast of happy glee,
In nature's palette, wild and free.

So come and join this bright parade,
Where joy and fun can't be delayed.
With every step, let laughter burst,
As we embrace this wonderous thirst.

Spore Dreams

In dreams of spores, we twirl and spin,
With laughter echoing from within.
A world of whimsy, dark and light,
With cap-topped friends, we take to flight.

Each tiny spore a tiny sage,
Unfolding tales from age to age.
With leaps of joy and hops of cheer,
In this enchanted land, we steer.

They ride on breezes, shake the leaves,
In every giggle, magic weaves.
A comic tale that never ends,
With wild delights and silly bends.

So close your eyes, let laughter bloom,
In spore dreams bright, you'll find your room.
Where joy and mischief intertwine,
A world of glee that's yours and mine.

The Laughter of Nature

Beneath the trees, a giggle grows,
A cap and stem in silly pose.
Bouncing spores that dance and twirl,
Nature's jesters in a swirl.

In puddles deep, they soak and play,
With colors bright to light the day.
They tickle toes as they abound,
In every nook, pure joy is found.

With giggles soft, they spread the cheer,
Each tiny hat brings smiles near.
Round every bend, a chuckle found,
A symphony of laughs around.

So join the fun beneath the shade,
Where silly antics never fade.
In this vast garden, let's partake,
Of laughter's light, for joy's own sake.

Microbial Merriment

In dampened soil, the sprites convene,
With pranks and jokes most unforeseen.
A pop of cap, a wiggly spin,
They turn the dark to grinning grin.

Tiny caps like hats, they wear,
Chasing shadows, light as air.
With whimsy sprouting from the ground,
A riddle in each giggle found.

They jive at dusk, they play at dawn,
In every patch, their laughter's drawn.
The earth supports this merry crew,
With every hue, a laugh rings true.

So let us join this fun parade,
Where every jest is unafraid.
Each little jest brings forth delight,
In twilight's glow, a sheer delight.

Hidden Joys of the Earth

In shady spots, the smiles peek,
With furry friends, we laugh and squeak.
A playful game on leafy beds,
Where whimsy sows its merry threads.

They wiggle up from damp and dark,
A playful trick, a joyful spark.
With every twist, the soil chuckles,
In nature's grip, the giggle buckles.

With plaid like suits and hats on heads,
They dance around where fun spreads.
A circle formed, they spin and sway,
In laughter's song, they lead the way.

So come and see these hidden smiles,
Within the wood, they fill the miles.
The earth is full of dainty fun,
With every step, the jest begun.

The Frolic in Foliage

Among the leaves, a merry sight,
With colors bold, they sprout with might.
A twirl, a leap, they know no fears,
A rollicking dance, they bring us cheer.

They wear their hats with such great flair,
A dimpled grin beyond compare.
In sunlit patches, frolic bright,
They tickle hearts with pure delight.

With each rich scent, a laugh will bloom,
Beneath the canopy's soft gloom.
Every shroom has tales to weave,
In their own world, we can't believe.

So take a breath, enjoy the scene,
In nature's joy, pure love is keen.
With laughter woven through each leaf,
Embrace the fun, let go of grief.

Colors of the Canopy

Beneath the trees where shadows dance,
Tiny caps in bright romance.
With polka dots and stripes galore,
They giggle softly, beg for more.

A yellow cap with a cheeky grin,
Says, "Join the party, let's begin!"
In this lush world, so wild and free,
Who knew the fun was here to see?

From red to brown, they sway and sway,
In the forest's vibrant cabaret.
With every laugh and playful cheer,
The canopy shakes; joy is near!

So gather round, and don't delay,
For nature's jesters are here to play.
With colors bright and mirthful lore,
We're lost in laughter forevermore.

Amino Acid Antics

In a petri dish, they start to glow,
Amino friends putting on a show.
They twist and tumble, a wacky dance,
In science class, they take their chance.

Proteins giggle, and enzymes tease,
With little quirks that aim to please.
"I'm a building block," one takes a bow,
While others chuckle, "Yeah, we know how!"

The lab coats laugh, their test tubes shake,
As amino pals start to awake.
In every corner, joy is found,
Where science sings and smiles abound.

So, watch them twirl in petri's light,
These quirky bonds bring such delight.
With every dip and joyful cheer,
The antics here are crystal clear!

Dappled Laughter

Amidst the leaves, a secret glee,
A patchwork quilt of jubilee.
With every sunbeam's playful tease,
They spread their joy among the trees.

In hidden glades, they laugh and play,
Creating scenes that brighten day.
Each little spot sings out with jest,
As sunlight gives the forest zest.

With cheeky winks, they disappear,
Then pop back up, spread laughter near.
Amongst the ferns, a giddy chase,
In nature's heart, they find their place.

So dappled joy, keep spreading wide,
In leafy realms where dreams abide.
We'll dance along this merry path,
In nature's laughter, find our math.

Mycelial Mischief

Beneath the soil, they plot and scheme,
Tiny threads with a playful dream.
They whisper secrets to the roots,
As laughter sprinkles like outshoots.

"Let's tickle those who walk above,"
Says one brave strand, "with purest love!"
They giggle soft with every sprout,
Creating joy in a sneaky route.

In every nook, they twist and turn,
With cheerful pranks that brightly burn.
They swirl in dance and tease the air,
A frolic found in fungi's lair.

So if you stroll in shaded trails,
Listen closely to their tales.
For mycelial winks and jests abound,
In every corner of the ground.

Glimmers in the Gloom

In shadows deep, a giggle stirs,
A funny cap where laughter purrs.
With spotted hats that sway and dance,
They tickle toes, a jolly chance.

They whisper jokes in the night air,
A fungal gang beyond compare.
With silly shapes and colors bright,
They light the dark with pure delight.

Underneath the leafy spread,
They craft their humor, laughter fed.
In every nook, a jest is found,
As echoed chuckles swell around.

So join the fun, don't miss the show,
With caps and caps that steal the glow.
In this bizarre, enchanted place,
The funny sprouts bring smiles to face.

Whimsical World Beneath

Beneath the trees, a realm so wry,
Where fungi prance and giggles fly.
Each tiny hat a dreamer's crown,
In humor's grip, they'll never frown.

They joke with bugs, a merry crowd,
Where laughter swells both bright and loud.
From silly shapes to colors bold,
These jests of nature never grow old.

They pop up here, they pop up there,
In every nook, they spark a flare.
With quirky stunts and playful cheer,
They keep the wonder ever near.

So step right in, enjoy the sight,
In this delight, the world feels light.
With every cap, a giddy scheme,
Join in the fun—embrace the dream!

Joyous Growth

From earth they rise, a hapless crowd,
With giggles bright, they're surely proud.
Each little sprout, a funny face,
In this odd patch, there's no disgrace.

They twist and twirl, a lively bunch,
With every step, you'll want to lunch.
On every stem, a joke is spun,
A garden full of glee and fun.

With hats so silly, they take a stand,
In this strange forest, all is grand.
You'll find them grinning, full of cheer,
Inviting all to draw near.

So laugh along, take heart, be spry,
In this joyous realm, we'll surely fly.
With every glance, surprise unfurls,
In growth and giggles, wonder swirls.

Spore Songs

In twilight's glow, the spore songs rise,
With giggles blaring 'neath the skies.
Each tiny puff a jolly tune,
That tickles fancy, makes hearts swoon.

They dance in circles, twist and spin,
With laughter's echo, we all begin.
In every note, a chuckle hides,
As nature's jesters take their rides.

From every cap, a story told,
Of silly antics, brave and bold.
In fields of green, they prance and play,
With each new dawn, they'll find a way.

So lend an ear to the funny sound,
In spore-studded air, we're joyfully bound.
Embrace the whimsy, join the spree,
In this bright world, let laughter be free.

www.ingramcontent.com/pod-product-compliance
Lightning Source LLC
Chambersburg PA
CBHW051701160426
43209CB00004B/979